Look at My Book

How Kids Can Write & Illustrate Terrific Books

written and illustrated by

Loreen Leedy

Holiday House ✿ New York

To all the teachers who encouraged me to write and draw

Copyright © 2004 by Loreen Leedy
All Rights Reserved
Printed and Bound in China
www.holidayhouse.com
5 7 9 10 8 6

Library of Congress Cataloging-in-Publication Data
Leedy, Loreen
Look at my book: how kids can write & illustrate terrific books / written and illustrated by Loreen Leedy—1st ed.
p. cm.
Summary: Provides ideas and simple directions
for writing, illustrating, designing, and binding books.
ISBN 0-8234-1590-2 (hardcover)
ISBN 0-8234-1959-2 (paperback)
1. Authorship—Juvenile literature. 2. Book design—Juvenile literature.
3. Illustration of books—Juvenile literature. 4. Handicraft.] I. Title.
[1. Authorship. 2. Book design. 3. Illustration of books. 4. Handicraft.] I. Title.
PN159.L44   2003
808'.02—dc21   2003041713
ISBN-13: 978-0-8234-1959-3 (pbk)

Dear Young Authors and Artists,

Have you ever made your own book? This book is full of ideas you can use when you write and illustrate your own stories. Use it as a general guide, and please ask a grown-up for help if you need it. When I start a book, I grab a pencil and some paper....Let's get going!

Loreen Leedy

ideas

The words and art in a book start with ideas.

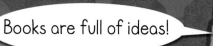

Books are full of ideas!

TIPS on getting ideas:

Read.

Ask questions.

Learn something new.

Listen to what people say.

Watch the world around you.

Think of how to improve things.

Invent an imaginary world.

Remember details.

Keep a journal.

Doodle.

And don't forget to . . .

Brainstorm!

I want to write an exciting story. Now what?

I want to write about birds, but I need more ideas.

I've got a great idea— a book about ME!

Brainstorming

means to think of a whole bunch of ideas.

Okay... what do I know about birds? I'll write down what I can think of.

Bird Food
sunflower seeds
peanuts
worms
bugs
fruit

Where Birds Live
birdhouse
hollow tree
bushes
cliffs
roofs

Bird Names
cardinal
hummingbird
blue jay
pigeon
eagle
owl

What would make an exciting story? Getting lost. Being chased. Snakes. Quicksand. Leaky boat. Treasure map...

quicksand   gold
swamp   climb tree   get lost   treasure
jungle   map   leaky boat
fall in hole   EXCITING STORY
                 snake
get chased
        alligator

Things about me: my favorite foods and toys, where I was born, my family, best tricks, fastest tail-wag...

Brainstorming TIPS:

1) **Make a list of your ideas.**

2) **Make an idea web.**

3) **Draw pictures.**

4) **Try to think of as many ideas as possible.**

5) **Think of weird ideas, boring ideas, silly ideas—**
   a "bad" idea might lead to a great one.

6) **Try brainstorming with another person or a group.**

7) **Write down each idea so you don't forget it.**

5

Characters can be real or imaginary.

can be people, animals, or something else....

I'm not real, on this planet, anyway!

All my characters are real birds.

I'm real, mostly.

An author invented me.

Me, too!

My character is a guy who has lots of adventures.

He could be an explorer. Or a treasure hunter. Or a scientist or...

I'm based on my author's uncle.

Character Ideas:
Astronaut
Dancer
Lizard
Robot
TV

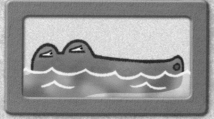

I'm imaginary, but you seem real.

GRROWWWLLL!!!

8

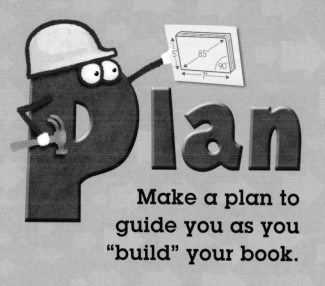

Plan

Make a plan to guide you as you "build" your book.

How can I make a plan? I don't even know what the story is yet!

Maybe making a plan will help you figure it out.

Start to imagine what could be in your book.

Make a list of what might be in your book.

This looks okay. I can always make changes later.

Title (Lindy's Birds?)
About the Author
Dedication
Penguins
Ducks
Ostriches
Hummingbirds
Cardinals
Owls
Toucans

Make a storyboard to plan the sequence of events. (It looks a lot like a comic strip.)

This is Zak. | He finds treasure map. | Flies his plane. | Arrives in swamp. | Gets into boat. | Boat sinks.

Wades to island. | Gets stuck in mud. | Grabs gator's tail. | Runs from gator. | Digs up old trunk. | It's full of r...

Try out different plans for your book. Which one do you like best?

Zak leaves for vaca...
He goes on a hike.
He gets lost in the...
A wild pig runs af...
He hides in a cav...
He finds a circle...
He lifts up a bi...
A rusty can is...
It's full of old...
Zak buys a boat an...
terrible weather, gets home.

Zak flies over a wilderness.
The fuel tank starts to leak.
He lands and starts walking.
He suddenly falls into a sinkhole.
A big bear skeleton falls on him.
He starts to dig himself out.
He finds an old gold coin.
He digs and digs for more.
He finds a wooden box.
It won't open, but it's heavy.
He takes it home and opens it.
It's full of worthless rocks.

Fiction Writing TIPS:

1) When you're writing a story, you need a good **plot**. (The plot is "what happens.") Give your story a beginning, a middle, and an end.

2) In most stories, the main character has a **problem**. What problem can you give to your character?

3) What **solution** is there? Get your character in trouble, then help him or her get out of trouble again.

Nonfiction Writing TIPS:

1) Nonfiction is based on **facts**. Find facts to include by doing research (see page 7).

2) Some ways to do research: Interview an expert. Visit a place in person. Watch an event. Look in books, CDs, videos, etc. Search on the Internet.

3) Take **notes** on what you find out. Also, take photographs and/or make sketches.

Rough draft

Your first try at writing the text for your book.

This is pretty messy, but it's okay for now.

TIPS for rough drafts:

1) Use your notes, lists, and plans to get started.
2) Write quickly. Don't try to get everything perfect at this stage.
3) Leave plenty of space between each line so you can scribble in new words as you go.
4) Have fun and experiment with your writing. You can always change any part of it later on.

Rough Sketches

The first step in making the art for your book.

TIPS for rough sketches:

1) Find a picture of the subject to use as a guide while you're drawing (optional).

2) Make simple line drawings of the characters and settings you plan to use. Don't try to make final art, just loose sketches for now.

3) Draw with short, light strokes. Don't press down on your pencil too hard.

Gators!

Gators!

Dad

Share

what you have so far and get suggestions.

How is your book coming along?

Zak dropped some nuts. The gator wouldn't leave.

…the gator was catching up, so Zak climbed up a tree. The gator lay down underneath. How do you get rid of an alligator? wondered Zak.

Why don't you put a dog in your story?

The dog could sniff out the treasure and dig it up and chase the gator and…

Maybe Zak gets lost for days and has to eat lizards and spiders!

What if after Zak finds the treasure, the gator eats it?

I like some of these ideas but not all of them.

Sharing TIPS:

1) Show your rough drafts and sketches to one person or a group.
2) Ask for ideas and suggestions about how you can make your book better.
3) Use the suggestions you like and make changes to your book.
4) If you don't like someone's idea, just ignore it.

Revise

means to rewrite.

Revising TIPS:

1) Add words and take out words.
2) Switch words around.
3) Use lively language.
4) Use specific words instead of general words.
5) Include interesting details.
6) Brainstorm again if you need to.
7) Do more research if you need to.

Edit means to fix mistakes.

Editing is scary!

It doesn't have to be.

I can help check spelling.

So can I.

Spell Checker

Dictionary

That should be a capital O.

That sentence needs a period at the end.

A Dog's Life by Harrison Fuzz

My first memory is of my mother licking my face. Her tongue was like a huge we beach towel. Sometimes when sh it felt like I was drowning.

It took me only a week to learn h wag my tail. Dad was so proud! yip the loudest and bite hardest, t sisters used to hide under the bed.

One of the scariest things we had to learn was how to walk down stair one time I really hurt my le I still limp a little when it rains The othe

Format

is the size and shape of your book.

Will your book be **big**?

Or small?

Square?

Horizontal?

Vertical?

Will your book have an interesting shape? (Keep the shape simple so it's easy to turn the pages.)

This looks like an alligator head, I think.

Try making a scroll.

Or make a zigzag-shaped book.

Your book could have flaps.

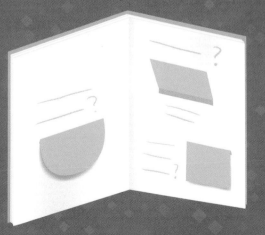

Or pockets.

Or pop-ups.

Layout

Sketch a design to figure out where the words and art will go on the pages.

One simple layout for a two-page spread is to put the words on one page and the art on the other.

Layout TIPS:

1) Write out the words by hand or use a computer printout to see how much space they take up.

2) Try putting the lines of words inside the art or curving them around the art.

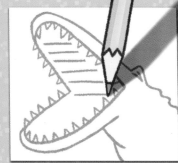

A book plan has layouts for all the pages of your book.

back cover   front cover   title page   spread

Your book can include one or more of these special pages:

Title page

An
Amazing
Story

written and illustrated
by Arthur Arteeste

Author page

Your Name
Age
Town
A Photograph
Interests
etc.

Copyright

©2010 by Your Name
(use current year)

Dedication

(For example:)
This book is
dedicated to
my Uncle Arf,
who taught me
how to howl.

Contents

Resources

(Make a list of
books, websites,
videos, clubs,
magazines, and
other sources for
readers to get
more information.)

Glossary

Glossary: a list
of key words
in your book
with definitions

Art

Pick a style for your book.

Speech bubbles: "What art style are you going to use in your book?" — "I'm not sure." — "Me neither."

Speech bubbles: "Are you a mouse?" — "Of course!" — "Me, too!" — "Why do we all look so different?" — "We each have our own style!"

Lines

| thick | smooth | jagged | dotted | lumpy | dark |
| thin | sketchy | wiggly | dashed | soft | light |

Shapes

| average | skinny | plump | rounded | distorted |

Patterns

| spots | checks | stripes | plaid | waves | zigzags |

24

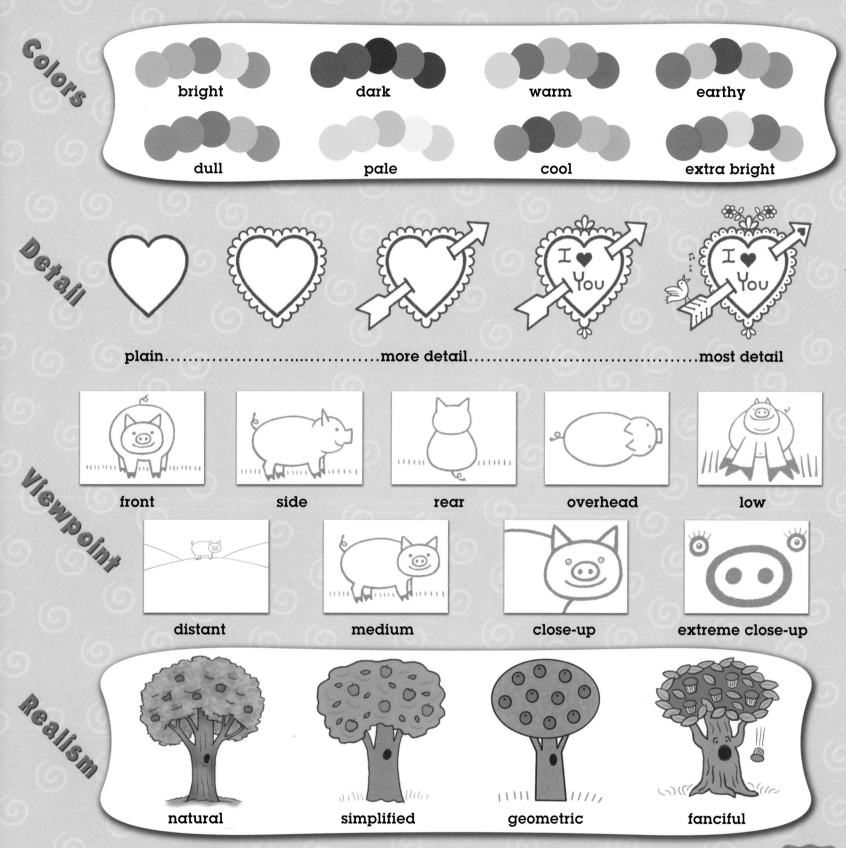

Colors

bright

dark

warm

earthy

dull

pale

cool

extra bright

Detail

plain……………………..……….more detail……………………………..……….most detail

Viewpoint

front

side

rear

overhead

low

distant

medium

close-up

extreme close-up

Realism

natural

simplified

geometric

fanciful

The lines, shapes, colors, and so on create the style of your book's **illustrations**.

Illustration TIPS:

1) Gather your text, sketches, and layouts.

2) Test your art supplies and paper. Use paper for your book's pages that works well with the art supplies. For example, paint watercolors on heavy paper.

3) Cut the paper to the size of your book's pages. Or work on larger paper and cut it to size later.

4) Lightly sketch in art and words with pencil. See page 28 for lettering ideas.

5) Apply art supplies (next page). Allow artwork to dry.

6) Erase any sketch lines that show.

There are many different art supplies you can use for your book's illustrations.

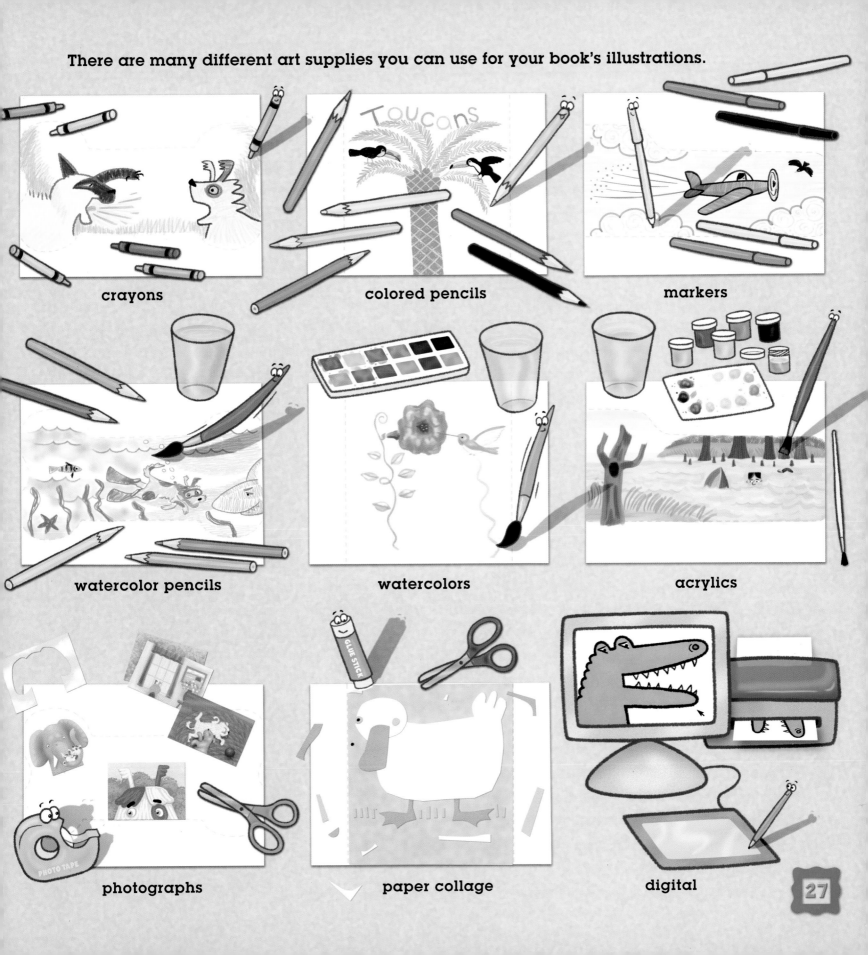

crayons

colored pencils

markers

watercolor pencils

watercolors

acrylics

photographs

paper collage

digital

Lettering

can be plain or decorative.

Lettering TIPS:

1) Use decorative letters for the title and plainer letters for the text.

2) Lightly draw in the letters with a pencil. Go over the lines with a gel pen, marker, or other tool.

Plain TALL Swirly **wide** ANGLED

Dotty Rough Flowery melting Spooky

Thorny Blobby wiggly holes Square

I just love fancy lettering.

This rubber stamp makes great "paw print" letters.

All my pages are finished—now I need to put them together.

My Favorite Feathered Friends

written + illustrated by Lindy Lane

A Dogs Life

MUDDY Millions

Binding holds a book's pages together.

Here are four easy ways to bind your book.

Yummy!

1) Measure and mark each hole. Each page needs at least two holes.

2) Make holes in one page at a time with a hole punch.

3) Tie pages and covers together with a shoelace, yarn, or string.

1) Gather the covers and pages. Line them up by tapping gently.

2) Staple in a straight row along the left edge.

1) Make a blank book by folding sheets of plain paper in half. Staple down the crease.

2) Attach art and text to each page with glue or tape.

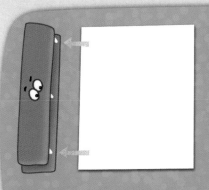

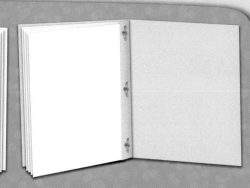

1) Punch holes in pages with a 3-hole punch.

2) Insert pages into a folder that has built-in paper fasteners.

3) Spread open paper fasteners to hold pages securely.

Examples

The possibilities are ENDLESS!

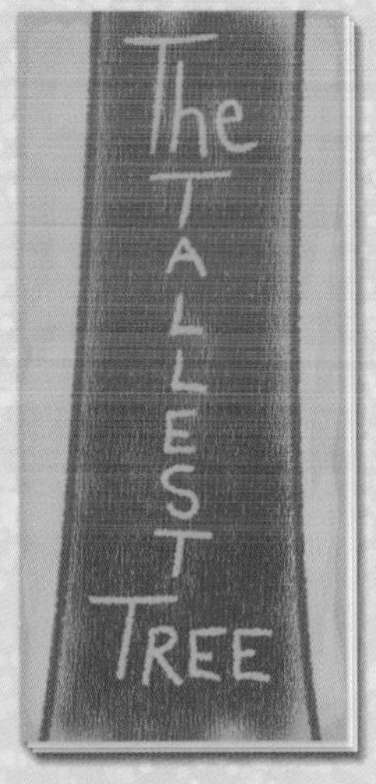

The Tallest Tree

Sam's Really Short Story

FISHY TALES

Cloud Zoo

The Unicorn in My Backyard

My Nature Journal

Peachy and the Soldier

Don't Eat the Mystery Meat! Advice for New Students

Look at my book!

OWLS

Spring!

30

ReSources

To find out more about making books, try looking here:

Learning to Write and Illustrate

Bang, Molly. **Picture This: How Pictures Work.** SeaStar Books, 2000. A professional illustrator shows how shapes and colors create a mood and tell a story.

Bauer, Marion Diane. **What's Your Story? A Young Person's Guide to Writing Fiction.** Clarion Books, 1992.

Christelow, Eileen. **What Do Illustrators Do?** Houghton Mifflin Co., 1997. Two artists use different art styles to illustrate the same story.
   What Do Writers Do? Houghton Mifflin Co., 1999. Two authors write different stories based on a similar incident.

Emberley, Ed. **Ed Emberley's Drawing Book of Animals.** Little Brown & Co., 1994 (reprint). One of many art books by the well-known author-illustrator with step-by-step directions for drawing a variety of critters.

Gee, Robyn. **What Shall I Draw?** EDC Publications, 1995. Step-by-step directions show how to draw a variety of items such as an owl, a rocket, and a dragon.

Hulme, Joy N. **How to Write, Recite, and Delight in All Kinds of Poetry.** Millbrook Press, 1996. Poems written by children are used as examples of various poetic forms.

Stevens, Janet. **From Pictures to Words: A Book About Making a Book.** Holiday House, 1995. A popular author-illustrator shows how she writes about and draws characters and settings to create a book.

Striker, Susan, with Edward Kimmel. **The Anti-Coloring Book: Creative Activities for Ages 6 and Up.** Owl Books, 2001. One of several books in a series that invite young artists to complete a drawing in a creative way.

Research Skills

Heiligman, Deborah. David Cain (illustrator). **The Kid's Guide to Research.** Scholastic Trade, 1999.

Souter, Gerry, Janet Souter, and Allison Souter. **Researching on the Internet Using Search Engines, Bulletin Boards, and Listservs.** Enslow Publishers, Inc., 2003.

Bookmaking

Diehn, Gwen. **Making Books That Fly, Fold, Wrap, Hide, Pop Up, Twist, and Turn.** Lark Books, 1998. Photographs and drawings show how to make a wide variety of books.

Valenta, Barbara. **Pop-O-Mania: How to Create Your Own Pop-ups.** Dial Books for Young Readers, 1997. Directions in three dimensions show readers how to create simple to complex pop-up books.

Getting Published

Henderson, Kathy. **The Young Writer's Guide to Getting Published.** Writers Digest Books, 2001 (6th edition).

Seuling, Barbara. **To Be a Writer: A Guide for Young People Who Want to Write and Publish.** Twenty-First Century Books, 1997.

Potluck: THE Magazine for the Serious Young Writer. A magazine that publishes work by young writers and artists. **www.potluck.org**

Stone Soup. A magazine that publishes work by young writers and artists. **www.stonesoup.com**

Word Dance. A magazine and website written for and by kids. **www.worddance.com.**

Zuzu. A magazine written and illustrated by children. **www.zuzu.org.**